I0214255

A Day At
Mr. McDoogle's Zoo

Written and Illustrated By:

Marie Whitton

Text and Illustrations Copyright © 2018 by Marie Whitton.
All rights reserved, including the right of reproduction in whole or in part in any form.
Book design by Marie Whitton

For My Husband
Greg

For My Children
Gregory, Ann-Marie &
Kimberly

For My
Grandchildren

Polar Bears

Gorillas

Toucans

Chimpanzee

Elephants

Penguins

Ostriches

Lions

Giraffes

Walruses

Zebras

Tigers

Camels

What a beautiful day for a trip to the zoo,
Looks like there will be much to see and do.
To Mr. McDoogle - "Hello" we did say,
Mr. McDoogle will show us the way.
There are animals of all kind,
From all over the world - we don't mind.
He will show off his zoo - for which he is proud,
Will we be wowed?

South American Flamingo

Flamingos - our first stop,
What beautiful colors - how they pop.
Their colors come from what they eat,
Which is in the water around their feet.

Australian
Kangaroo
&
Platypus

Kangaroos will hop - not walk,
That is the talk?
They hop so high into the sky,
They have powerful legs - that is why.

Platypus - is what we are seeing.
It sure is a strange being.
Has webbed feet, beaver like tail
and a duck bill,
Has fur like an otter and lays eggs - it will.

In the tropics the parrots live,
To us - a show - they will give.
Parrots are very smart birds,
Listen - you can hear words.

South American Parrots

Around the corner - look what we have found,
The noisiet birds - in the jungle - this is their sound.
For their colorful bills - toucans are known,
The longest bill of any bird in the world they are alone.

South American
Toucans

Mr. McDoogle - what do we hear?
Elephants are near.
They are the largest land animal on earth.
One elephant - at a time - to give birth.
The baby elephants love to play,
They will play all day.

African Elephants

The ostriches - here - we did find,
The largest bird in the world -
of it's kind.
Ostriches are too big to fly,
They are too heavy - this is why.

African
Ostriches

African
Zebras

Camels

Camels live in the sandy desert so very hot,
Water - there is not.
On their backs - see the bump?
They store fatty tissues in their hump.
It changes to water or energy -
this is prime,
So - camels can survive without food or
water for a long time.

Look over there,
Zebras are running in two pair.

African Giraffes

Giraffes are the tallest animals of the land,
Taller than trees - do they stand.
Always eating leaves from that tree,
With their long necks - they reach what they see.

African
Lions

Around the corner we heard the lions roar,
One can tell they were not bored.
The lion is the second largest cat,
This cat we cannot pat.

Asian
Tigers

Larger than a lion is a tiger - another cat,
This too - we will not pat.
Tigers are good swimmers - we are told,
And good hunters - they are very bold.

Mr. McDoogle - would you tell us about these,
Chimpanzees and Gorillas - Please.
Very smart animals for the most,
Of this we can boast.
They are easy to teach,
Using rocks and sticks as tools to
reach.
African
Chimpanzee

African Gorillas

Hippopotamus means river horse,
Their skin is very coarse.
Third largest animal of our land,
Here is where they stand.
Hippos spend their time in a river or
swamp,
This is where they like to romp.

Asian
Hippopotamus

Rhinoceros means Nose Horn,
With horn stubs - they are born.
The second largest animal of the land -
Rhinos of white,
At over 7,000 pounds - they are not light.

Asian
Rhinoceros

To see the walruses - here we will go,
Mr. McDoogle- can you tell us about walruses - what do you know?
Loudly - they do bellow,
Walruses are not mellow.
In the cold waters of the Artic is where they live,
Shell fish to quench their hunger is what we will give.

Arctic
Polar Bears

Gaze over there,
It is a polar bear.
Largest meat eater that lives on land,
He is so very grand.
Spending most of their time at sea,
In the Artic is their favorite place to be.
What is their favorite meal?
That would be a seal.

Antarctica
Penguins

Penguins are birds,
These are the words.
Flippers for swimming - they cannot fly,
That is how they get by.

To the reptile area - next - is where we will go,
Reptiles are turtles, snakes, lizards, and alligators - this we know.
Almost all reptiles will lay eggs,
And not all have legs.
All have to heat up with the sun of the day,
Cold blooded are they.

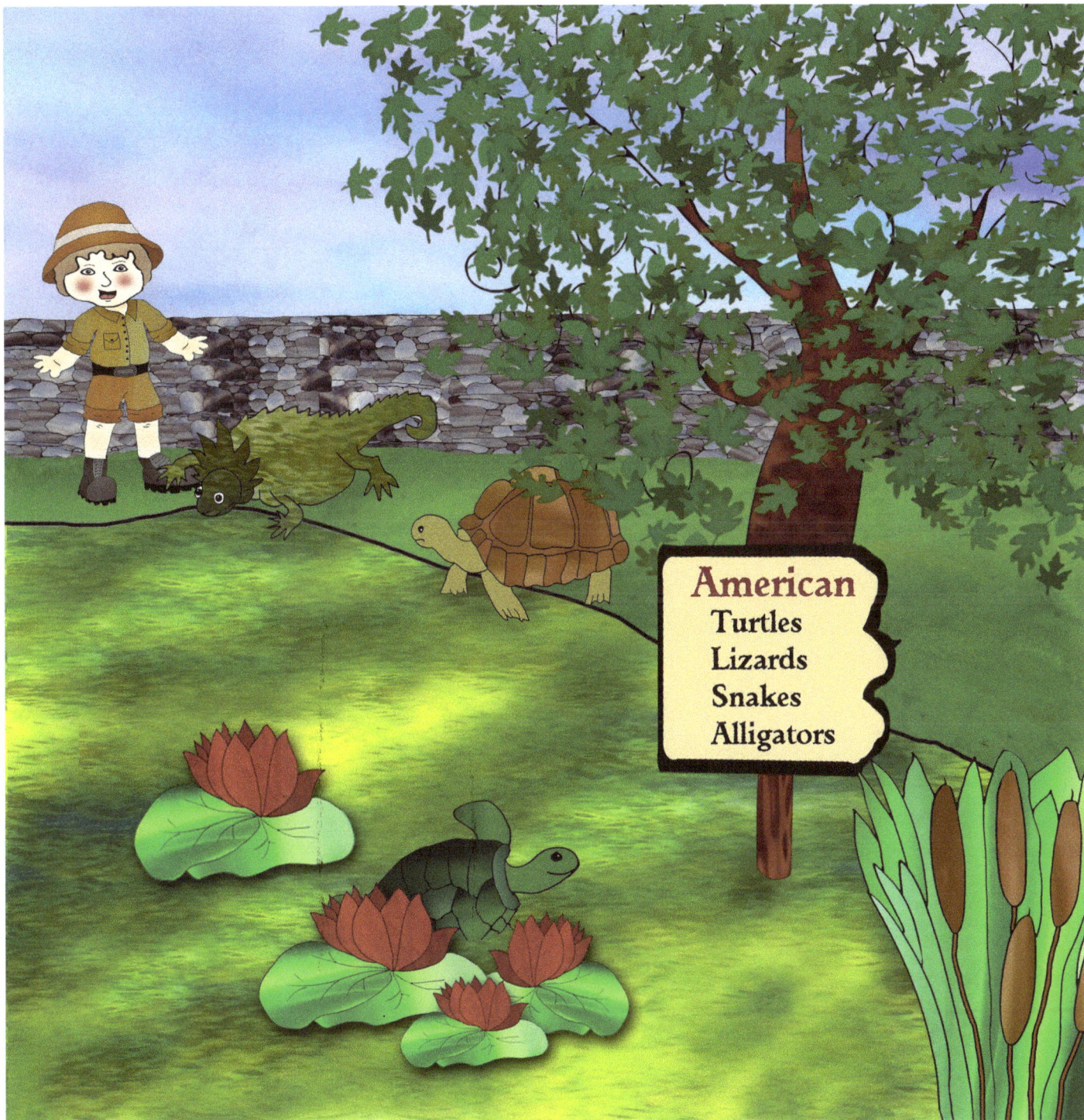

American
Turtles
Lizards
Snakes
Alligators

American
Black Bear
Ringtail Cat
Rabbit
Armadillo
Coyote
Owl
Vulture

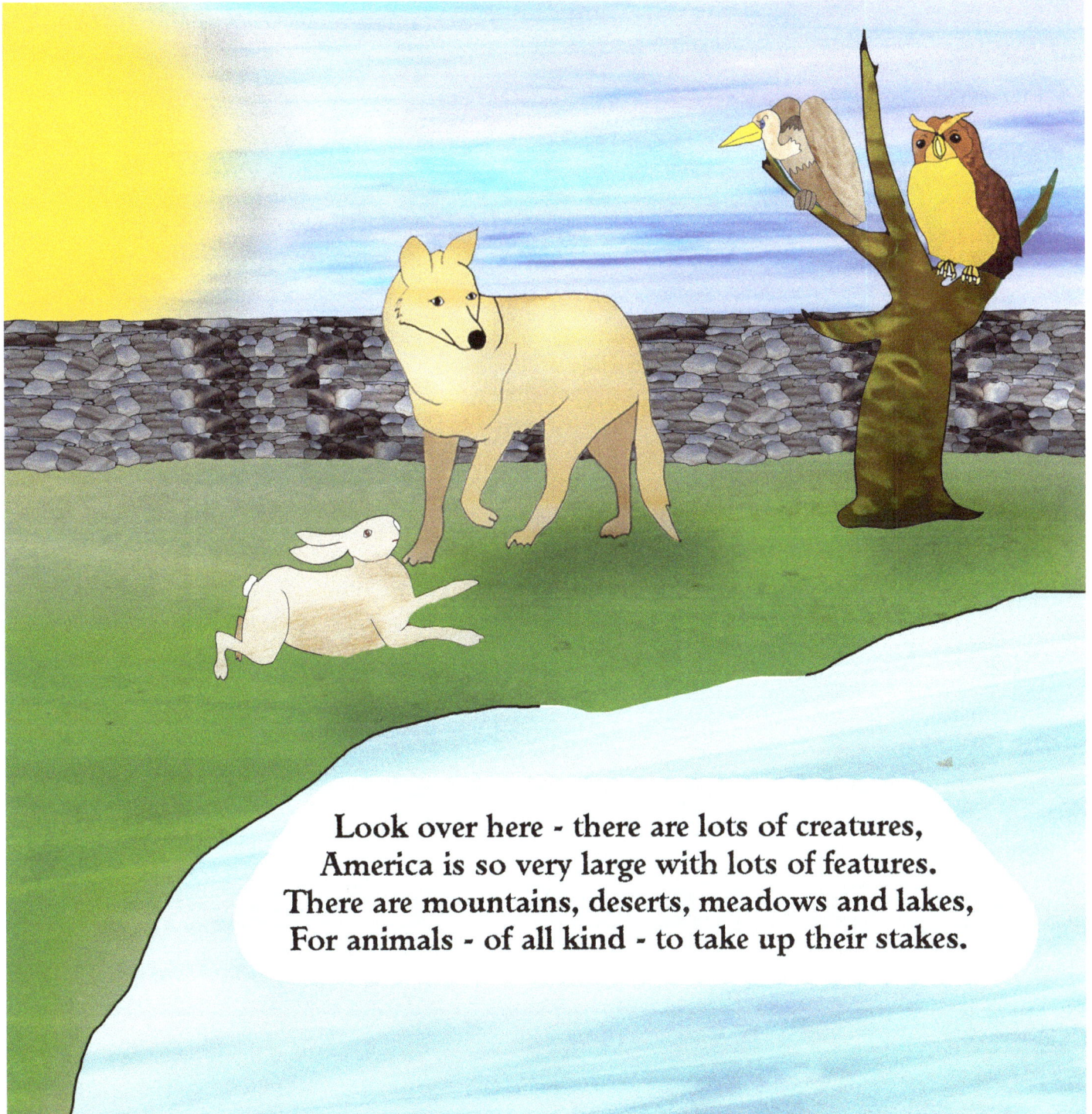

Look over here - there are lots of creatures,
America is so very large with lots of features.
There are mountains, deserts, meadows and lakes,
For animals - of all kind - to take up their stakes.

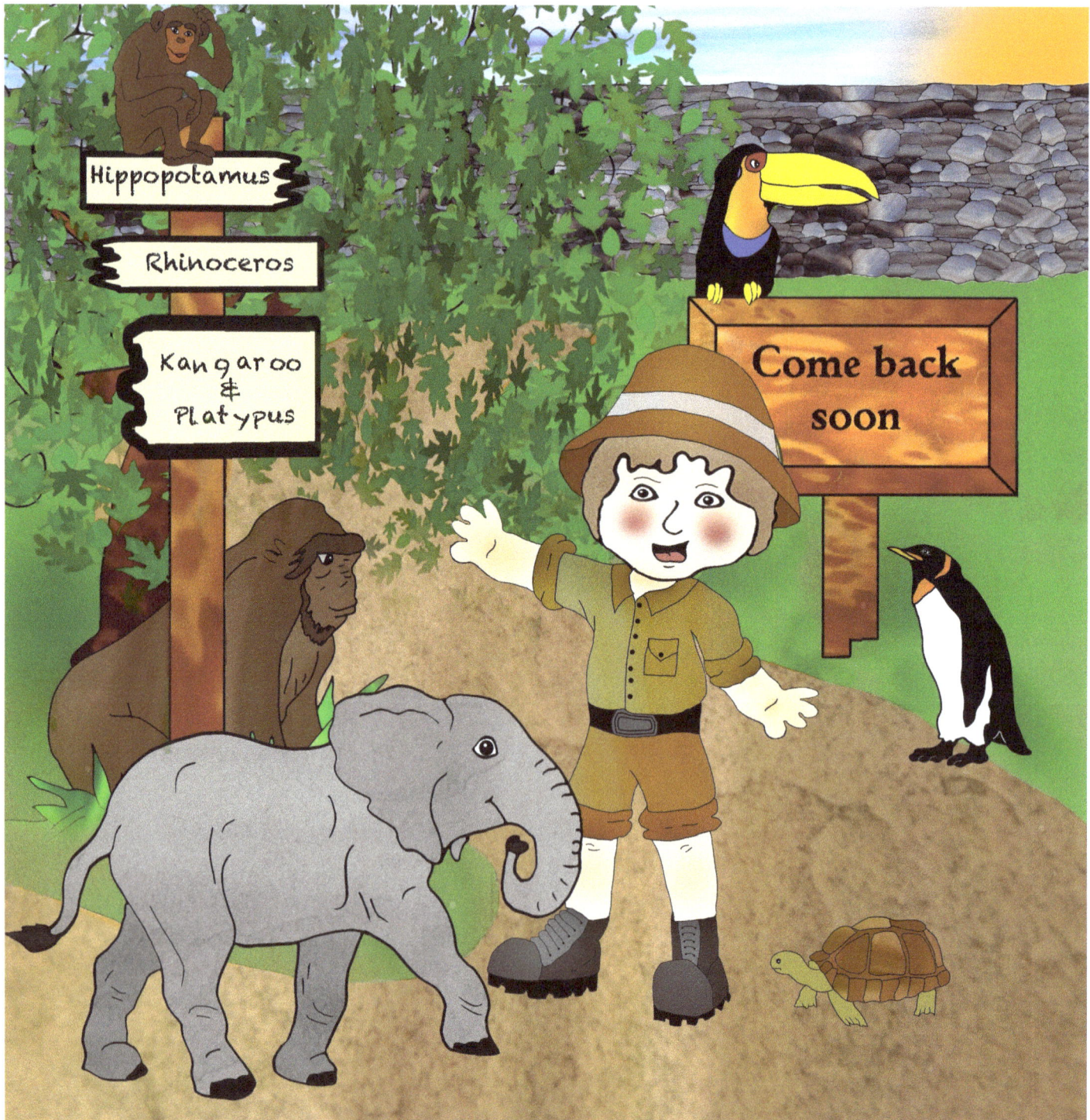

Polar Bears

Gorillas

Toucans

Chimpanzee

Elephants

Penguin

Ostriches

Lions

Giraffe

Walruses

Zebras

Camels

Tigers

It sure was a beautiful day for a trip to the zoo,
There was so much to see and do.
To Mr. McDoogle -"Thank you" we did say,
We will have to come back another day.
He did show us his zoo - for which he was proud,
We certainly were wowed.